THE TULSA RACE MASSACRE

"Even before Dr. Martin Luther King Jr.
was alive to dream his dream,
Black folks in Tulsa, Oklahoma
in the Greenwood District
were already overcoming."
— Phetote Mshairi

BY KARA L. LAUGHLIN

Published by The Child's World®
1980 Lookout Drive, Mankato, MN 56003-1705
800-599-READ • www.childsworld.com

PHOTOS
Cover and page 4: Alvin C. Krupnick Co./Library of
Congress, Prints and Photographs Division
Interior: Alvin C. Krupnick Co./Library of Congress, Prints and Photographs Division:
19, 28; AP Photo/Sue Ogrocki: 27, 31; Collection of the Smithsonian National Museum
of African American History and Culture, Gift of the Families of Anita Williams
Christopher and David Owen Williams: 8; Everett Collection/Newscom: 17; Everett
Collection/Shutterstock.com: 12, 14; John Vachon/Library of Congress, Prints and
Photographs Division: 7; Leemage/UIG Universal Images Group/Newscom: 15;
Library of Congress, Prints and Photographs Division: 6, 13, 21, 24, 25, 29 (both);
North Wind Picture Archives: 5; Oklahoma Historical Society/Archive Photos via
Getty Images: 23; Schomburg Center for Research in Black Culture, Jean Blackwell
Hutson Research and Reference Division, The New York Public Library: 11

LIBRARY OF CONGRESS CATALOGING-IN-PUBLICATION DATA
ISBN 9781503853713 (Reinforced Library Binding)
ISBN 9781503854093 (Portable Document Format)
ISBN 9781503854215 (Online Multi-user eBook)
LCCN: 2020943350

Printed in the United States of America

Cover and page 4 caption:
Smoke billows from
buildings during the 1921
Tulsa Race Massacre

CONTENTS

Chapter One

A PLACE TO BE FREE

In 1906, America was no easy place for Black Americans. The 13th, 14th, and 15th **Amendments** to the Constitution had been law for thirty years. Formerly enslaved people were free citizens, and Black men had the right to vote. But the white families who had bought and sold African Americans like farm equipment didn't feel bound by the law. Neither did many whites who never owned enslaved workers. Being called free and being free were two very different things.

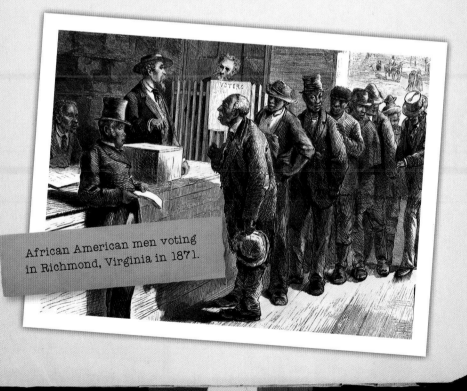

African American men voting in Richmond, Virginia in 1871.

Ottowa W. (O.W.) Gurley knew this firsthand. Mr. Gurley was a teacher and grocer born to formerly enslaved parents. He knew that there were few places where Black Americans could improve their lives. Mr. Gurley moved to Oklahoma to take part in the **Land Run of 1889**. In 1906, he purchased 40 acres (16 ha) of land just outside the growing town of Tulsa, Oklahoma. He planned to divide it up and sell it. Mr. Gurley planned to give Black people a chance almost unheard-of in the U.S. at that time: a chance to own land.

In 1906 it was just about impossible for Black people to buy property. Even though Black Americans were full citizens by law, white people held all the property. Most wouldn't sell to Black people. White people also had most of the power. They used it to pass laws that kept Black people from the same opportunities as white people. These were known as **Jim Crow laws**.

Black Americans picking cotton in 1907.

COLORED

A Black boy at a water fountain labeled for use by "colored" people only.

Greenwood around 1920.

Mr. Gurley built a grocery store and rooming house so that newcomers would have a place to live. He built them on a road along the railroad tracks that formed one boundary of his property. Many of the first boarders were from a town in Mississippi called Greenwood. He named the road Greenwood Avenue. Eventually Greenwood became the name for the whole town.

John the Baptist (J.B.) Stradford also purchased land outside of Tulsa. Like Mr. Gurley, he believed that owning businesses was the key to getting ahead. Together, the men built stores, rental properties and other businesses. Mr. Stradford ran a 54-room hotel in Greenwood. At that time, it was the largest Black-owned hotel in the United States.

Both men worked together to grow Greenwood. They sold land to other Black people, where they could build homes and businesses. They rented homes to others. They lent money to people starting new ventures. They began to grow a town where Black people could thrive—without needing permission from white people to do it.

They could not have chosen a better location. Oil had been discovered in Oklahoma, and Tulsa was growing quickly to support the oil industry. In 1910, Greenwood was **annexed** onto the growing boomtown of Tulsa.

O. W. Gurley and J. B. Stradford went by their initials for a reason. In the west, white men called each other by their last names, but boys were called by their first names. Often, white men would call Black men by their first names as a way of trying to make them feel like boys instead of men. Mr. Gurley and Mr. Stradford used their initials as a way of protesting and trying to prevent that practice.

Mr. Gurley named the street where his grocery and rooming houses were located Greenwood Avenue. Many early residents of Greenwood were fleeing lynchings and racial violence from Greenwood, Mississippi.

As Tulsa grew, so did Greenwood. Soon, Greenwood had dress shops, hair dressers, and theaters. By 1920, Greenwood was home to 108 Black-owned businesses. There were 41 grocery stores, 30 places to eat, two movie theaters, two different newspapers, and dozens of professional offices. It was also home to 22 churches, a public library, and an excellent school.

There was a thriving music scene, especially for jazz and blues. Count Basie, who would later conduct a famous jazz band, first heard jazz as a young man in Greenwood. Greenwood was home to many of the wealthiest Black Americans. Jewelry stores and fur shops opened to serve these customers. Greenwood came to be known as **Black Wall Street**, a metaphor first used by Booker T. Washington and still used today.

Not everyone who lived in Greenwood was wealthy. In addition to the doctors, lawyers, and business owners, Greenwood was also home to janitors, dishwashers and maids. Some lived in the rooming houses near the railroad track. Others lived in shacks and shanties and struggled to get by. Only the wealthiest could live along "Professor's Row" in the fine houses that drew the envy of white Tulsans.

Chapter Two

A CITY DIVIDED

Jim Crow laws throughout the United States enforced the
segregation of Black and white people. Tulsa was no exception.
Oklahoma became a state in 1907. The state's very first law,
Senate Bill Number 1, banned Black people from "residing,
traveling and marrying outside their race."

Black Tulsans could not walk into stores or restaurants
that served white customers. They couldn't live next to white
neighbors. They couldn't even travel in the same cars on trains. If
African Americans wanted to go out to eat, buy groceries or stay
in Tulsa overnight, they had to do it in Greenwood. So they did.

Only white people
were welcome at this
shop in Atlanta.

These Black men were all awarded medals in World War I (1914-1918)

Tulsa in 1909.

Black workers would make their money working in the white areas of Tulsa, then spend their money in Greenwood. It's been said that every dollar spent in Greenwood was re-spent in the community many times over. The people of Greenwood couldn't help but invest in their community.

Greenwood's success didn't sit well with many of the white residents of Tulsa. Just as Greenwood had low-wage workers, areas with more white residents of Tulsa also had plenty of citizens working for low wages in difficult conditions. They didn't like seeing Black people doing better for themselves than they were doing.

Throughout the United States, many white people were still unhappy about **emancipation**. They didn't believe Black people were as good as white people. They resented seeing Black people who seemed successful while they themselves were struggling. White servicemen returned from the first World War to discover Black men employed in their old jobs. Black veterans came home to find they were not treated with gratitude for serving in the war, but resented for having succeeded when white people had said they wouldn't.

Resentment, anger over uncertain economic times, and entrenched racist ideas contributed to tension and violence. In the summer of 1919, now known as the **Red Summer**, racial violence erupted in cities throughout the country, including violent attacks in Chicago, Omaha, and Washington, DC. Racist hate groups, especially the **Ku Klux Klan** (KKK), controlled state and local governments in many states, including Oklahoma. In the two years following the end of the war, the KKK was responsible for more than 150 lynchings throughout the U.S., mostly of Black men and women.

A KKK meeting near Washington DC in 1921.

One such lynching happened in Greenwood in August of 1920. A young white man named Roy Belton was being held in the Tulsa courthouse for shooting a taxi driver. On the night after his arrest, articles in the white-owned newspapers called for a lynching. A **mob** entered the courthouse and demanded that the sheriff hand Belton over to them. Later the boy was found hanging from a tree. This tragic event was in the mind of many Tulsans nine months later, when two accidents would set off one of the worst acts of racial violence the country had yet seen.

Chapter Three

VIOLENCE IN GREENWOOD

The first accident happened on May 30, 1921.

A 19-year-old Black shoe shiner named Dick Rowland entered an elevator with Sarah Page, a white, 17-year-old elevator operator. Though the details are unclear, it seems that Dick Rowland tripped getting into the elevator. He reached out and grabbed Sarah Page's arm to break his fall. When he did, Sarah Page screamed.

In Tulsa, in 1921, when a white woman screamed in the presence of a Black man, there were plenty of white people around willing to turn it into trouble. Mr. Rowland knew this, so he ran.

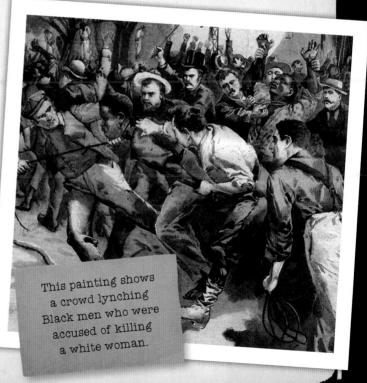

This painting shows a crowd lynching Black men who were accused of killing a white woman.

On May 31, Dick Rowland was arrested and taken to the courthouse—the same courthouse where Roy Belton had met his terrible end less than a year before. That night an article about the arrest was published in one of Tulsa's white newspapers, the *Tulsa Tribune*. The article wrongly accused Rowland of attacking Sarah Page.

Survivors of the massacre tell of an **editorial** calling for a lynching. No complete copy of the paper can be found. If those memories are correct, the editorial has been lost to history.

Even without such an editorial, the use of the word **assault** on the front page was enough to rile people up. "Assault" was a code word understood to mean an attack of a sexual nature. Many Black men throughout the south had been killed based on that kind of accusation. The residents of Greenwood had no reason to think things would be any different for Mr. Rowland.

Throughout the south, it was not safe to be a Black person. Lynchings and racial intimidation occurred across the country. Most lynchings happened in southern states. Many formerly enslaved people were moving to Oklahoma to escape unsafe conditions at home.

The *Tulsa Star*, a Black-owned paper, reported rumors of a planned lynching. An article called for Black people to arm themselves and defend their rights.

The newspaper articles stirred people to action. A group of 75 Black veterans took their guns to the courthouse to guard it. A mob of over 1,000 white people also arrived at the courthouse. They began shouting at the sheriff, demanding that he release Rowland into their hands. On seeing armed Black men, white men stole shotguns and ammunition from nearby stores.

Then came the second accident.

Chapter Four

THE ATTACK ON GREENWOOD

The veterans in front of the courthouse were told to leave. As they walked away from the courthouse, one member of the white mob grabbed at one of the veteran's guns. Two men scuffled. In the struggle, the gun fired.

When the gunshot rang out, it was like a starting pistol. It was like the moment in an action movie when someone drops a lit match on a floor covered in gasoline. Everything exploded. The streets erupted in gunfire and violence.

Fires began to erupt all over Greenwood as the violence grew.

The veterans fought the mob as they retreated toward Greenwood. In the early morning hours of June 1, the mob of white Tulsans throbbed into the streets of Greenwood. Some reports estimate that by daybreak, 10,000 white Tulsans were coming into Greenwood. Some shot at Greenwood residents. Others went block by block, **looting** and then setting fire to every shop and home. Planes began to fly above Greenwood. Some witnesses saw them dropping flaming balls of turpentine from the sky.

Some Greenwood residents shot back. Many others ran for their lives, seeking safety in the northern part of town.

The violence spread throughout Greenwood. Lawyer Buck Colbert Franklin wrote this about the night of May 31:

"I could see planes circling in mid-air. They grew in number and hummed, darted, and dipped low. I could hear something like hail falling upon the top of my office building. Down East Archer, I saw the old Mid-Way hotel on fire, burning from its top, and then another and another and another building began to burn from their top."

He described the crowd as well:

"On they rushed, whooping to the tops of their voices, firing their guns every step they took."

As they watched their homes and business burn, the people of Greenwood wondered where Tulsa's fine fire department was. But fire trucks never came. Instead of arresting the white people stealing, shooting and destroying the neighborhood, police officers rounded up and arrested the residents of Greenwood.

The violence lasted well into the next day. The police chief "deputized" five hundred white men, chosen from the mob that was calling for a lynching. He gave them weapons, and told them to deal with the situation as they saw fit. They saw fit to kill the Black residents of Greenwood. They broke into Greenwood's stores and homes, and stole valuables before setting the buildings on fire.

At 11:30 a.m. on June 1, Governor James Robertson declared **martial law**. The National Guard was called in to end the violence and restore order. Their main focus was on rounding up and jailing all Black citizens of Greenwood. Meanwhile, white Tulsans continued to torch the homes and businesses of Greenwood, which were now undefended.

Soldiers carrying away Black men after the violence ended.

By the morning of June 2, 1,256 houses in a 36-square-block area had been burnt to the ground. At the time, it was estimated that 36 people had died. Today it's believed that the actual figure is probably closer to 300 dead, most of them Black citizens. More than eight hundred people were wounded.

There were so many wounded that the Black hospital in Greenwood filled all of its beds. When it did, white hospitals in the city refused to admit Black patients. Greenwood's most prominent surgeon, A.C. Jackson, bled to death, unable to get into a hospital. He was shot in front of his own home, trying to surrender.

"The riot cheated us out of our childhood innocence," said Beulah Loree Keenan Smith, born in 1908. "My mother lost everything she owned," said Thelma Thurman Knight, born in 1915. "That riot was like a first 'war experience' for me," said World War II veteran Joe Burns, born in 1917.

—*The Ringer* article

Overnight, citizens went from wealthy to penniless. Mr. Gurley lost $200,000 in property, (worth 2.6 million today). Mr. Stradford's hotel, which had been worth $75,000 (over 1 million in today's money) was gone. In all, two million dollars of property was destroyed, an amount that would be worth almost 30 million dollars today. Black Wall Street was gone.

Greenwood's more than 10,000 citizens were largely homeless. More than 6000 were rounded up and put in **detention camps** at the county fairgrounds. Any Black person who didn't have a white employer to claim them was forced to clean up the destruction of Greenwood. Mayor T. D. Evans threated to arrest anyone who refused.

When Governor Robertson lifted martial law, Maurice Willows, an official with the American Red Cross, went to Greenwood. The Red Cross provides relief after storms and earthquakes. Willows persuaded the Red Cross to declare Tulsa a natural disaster area. He stayed and offered to help. The Mayor put the Red Cross in charge of helping the people of Greenwood. The city provided no money.

Chapter Five

A FAILURE OF JUSTICE

On June 3, the United States Attorney General ordered an investigation. The Governor of Oklahoma directed his Attorney General to investigate and save evidence for a grand jury. But in Tulsa, people were already making up stories about what had happened in Greenwood. The mayor, faith leaders and other officials were saying the residents of Greenwood had been responsible for the massacre. City officials, many of whom were members of the Ku Klux Klan, buried the truth of what had happened.

Greenwood was left in smoking ruins after the violence.

The grand jury determined that the mob of white people who had gathered outside the courthouse were just onlookers. They were not held responsible for the violence and looting that occurred. A state's attorney granted **immunity** to the white people who had participated in the massacre.

The city promised to pay for the damage, but the money never came. No insurance payments came either, since the insurers used "riot clauses," to refuse to pay. Only the American Red Cross helped the people of Greenwood to survive until they could rebuild.

Shortly after the massacre, some white Tulsans saw an opportunity. They decided they didn't want Greenwood to be rebuilt. Instead they passed laws that made rebuilding expensive and difficult. They tried to get Greenwood landowners to sell their property at low prices.

Some of Greenwood's most prominent residents, fleeing jail or violence, left Tulsa for good. Mr. Gurley fled to California. J.B. Stradford moved to Chicago. Publisher A.J. Smitherman escaped to Massachusetts with his family.

Many Greenwood residents stayed to rebuild, however. Maurice Willows promised to help anyone arrested for rebuilding. Several Greenwood lawyers sued over the zoning laws. The laws were found to be unfair, and the people of Greenwood were finally able to rebuild.

Within five years of the massacre, Greenwood had a thriving business district. By 1942, Greenwood was once again home to more than two hundred Black-owned businesses.

People searching through rubble for their belongings after the violence.

But many people never recovered what they had lost. It's said that years after the massacre, Black women would be walking down the street, seeing their jewelry on the necks of white women.

When we learn about an event as atrocious as the Greenwood Massacre, it's natural to want it to be an exception. Unfortunately, in the years after WWI many other Black communities around the United States suffered similar violence.

It was a common pattern. A group of Black citizens would begin to thrive. Their success would draw envy and hostility from whites in the community. A white person would accuse a Black man of a crime—frequently of assaulting a white woman. With tension already high, the white citizens would use the "crime" as an excuse to riot. During the Red Summer, there were two dozen such race massacres and almost one hundred lynchings.

It was rare for the white people who perpetrated these attacks to be punished. Black people were almost always jailed or killed for any white lives that were lost.

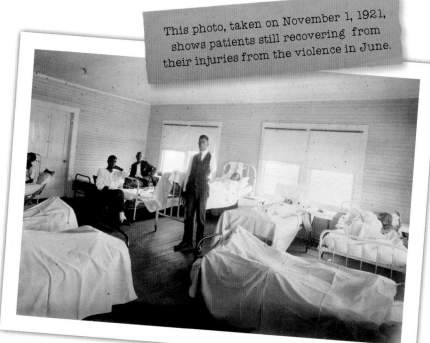

This photo, taken on November 1, 1921, shows patients still recovering from their injuries from the violence in June.

Chapter Six

GREENWOOD TODAY

For a long time, the story of the Greenwood massacre was not told. Local officials in Tulsa removed all mention of the massacre from history books. Children growing up in Greenwood didn't hear about it at school. The rest of the country also let the truth be covered by time and shame. But that silence has been broken.

A refugee camp was set up at the fairgrounds in Tulsa after the June violence.

In the 1970s, several writers began investigating the story of the massacre. Their writings brought new attention to the events. More books and articles followed. In 1997, the state of Oklahoma created a commission to study the massacre. After four years, they released a 200-page official report telling the truth about what happened in Greenwood. Today many local and national organizations are sharing the truth about the Greenwood Massacre.

In some ways, the story of Black Wall Street is still being told. Recent efforts to find mass graves from the time of the massacre have so far not been successful. **Reparations**, though recommended by the commission, have not come to pass. And Tulsa remains one of the most racially segregated cities in the United States.

On August 21, 2020, the people of Greenwood broke ground for a new museum called "Greenwood Rising," which will tell the story of Greenwood before, during and after the massacre, as well as Greenwood today and in the future.

The story of Black Wall Street is America's story. It's the story of people who worked hard to make a good life for themselves. It is also the story of the destructive power of a country divided against itself. And it is the story of people who refused to believe they were unworthy of dignity and opportunity.

The people of Greenwood faced enormous tragedy and vicious brutality. Everything was taken from them. They were never given any repayment for that theft. In the face of this horror and grave injustice, they worked together to recreate a place where they could live and thrive. They are an inspiration to all people living in the face of brutality, racism, and hate.

1921
BLACK WALL STREET
MEMORIAL

AFTER STATEHOOD, TULSA'S BLACK COMMUNITY, THROUGH RESOURCEFULNESS, SPIRIT, AND SELF-SUFFICIENCY, DEVELOPED A VIBRANT SHOWCASE OF AFRICAN-AMERICAN SUCCESS. AROUND THE INTERSECTION OF GREENWOOD AVENUE AND ARCHER STREET, BLACK-OWNED BUSINESSES LINED THE STREETS AND BROUGHT UNHERALDED WEALTH TO THE COMMUNITY, EARNING THE NAME, THE BLACK WALL STREET OF AMERICA. ARCHER STREET, ON THE BOUNDARY BETWEEN THE BLACK AND WHITE WORLDS, WAS THE IRONIC SYMBOL OF BOTH PROSPERITY AND OPPRESSION. WHILE SEGREGATION CREATED A VITAL ECONOMIC CENTER FOR BLACKS, IT CONFINED THEIR PLACE IN THE NATION, THE STATE, AND THE CITY.

THE GREENWOOD AREA SUFFERED THE MOST DEVASTATING SINGLE INCIDENT OF RACIST VIOLENCE IN THE 20TH CENTURY. ON JUNE 1, 1921, FOLLOWING A DISTORTED NEWSPAPER REPORT OF ASSAULT. IN 24 HOURS, AS MANY AS 300 BLACK CITIZENS DIED, AND 35 SQUARE BLOCKS, 23 CHURCHES, AND MORE THAN 2,000 BUSINESSES AND HOMES WENT UP IN FLAMES. A THICK, GRAY PALL HUNG OVER TULSA'S NORTHERN HORIZON FOR DAYS AS A RESULT OF THE MASSIVE FIRE. WITH HANDS RAISED BEFORE THE GUNS OF SOLDIERS, AN ESTIMATED 6,000 BLACK MEN, WOMEN, AND CHILDREN TRUDGED PAST GREENWOOD AND ARCHER STREETS TO TEMPORARY INTERNMENT CAMPS.

FIRE AND HATRED HAD DESTROYED THEIR COMMUNITY, BUT NOT THEIR ENTERPRISING SPIRIT. TULSA'S BLACK CITIZENS REBUILT THIS FAMED BUSINESS AVENUE MORE ENTERPRISING THAN BEFORE. THE TRAGIC INCIDENT OF 1921 BECAME THE NEW BEGINNING. THIS BLACK WALL STREET MEMORIAL IS DEDICATED TO THE ENTREPRENEURS, THE PIONEERS, AND TO GREENWOOD AVENUE'S RENAISSANCE. IT MARKS THE PAST, THE PRESENT, AND THE FUTURE. THE ETERNAL FLAME SYMBOLIZES, NOT MOURNING, BUT THE RESILIENCE OF A PEOPLE. THE FOUNTAIN SANCTIFIES THOSE PIONEERING SOULS WHO REFUSED TO RELINQUISH THEIR DREAM. THE BLACK WALL STREET MEMORIAL REACHES FOR THE UNITY OF ALL GOD'S PEOPLE.

STATE REPRESENTATIVE DON ROSS
GREENWOOD CULTURAL CENTER
A FOUNDER
1996

THE GREENWOOD CULTURAL CENTER, INC.
BOARD OF DIRECTORS
GRATEFULLY ACKNOWLEDGES THE CONTRIBUTIONS AND SUPPORT OF:
STATE REPRESENTATIVE DON ROSS • STATE SENATOR MAXINE HORNER
MAYOR M. SUSAN SAVAGE • CARVER MIDDLE SCHOOL
RODGER RANDLE, PRESIDENT • UNIVERSITY CENTER AT TULSA
JEWISH FEDERATION OF TULSA • @ SOUTHWESTERN BELL
STATE ARTS COUNCIL OF OKLAHOMA

1921 RACE RIOT DESTRUCTION DAMAGE CLAIMS

A memorial now stands to honor the people lost in the violence of the Tulsa Race Massacre.

**What were the advantages and disadvantages
to being a poor white person in Tulsa in the 1920s?
Compare this to those of a wealthy Black resident
of Greenwood during that same time.**
How do those advantages and disadvantages compare
to the lives of white and Black people today?

**The *Tulsa Tribune* used the word "assault" to describe
what happened between Dick Rowland and Sarah Page.**
How do words have power?
Does it matter if the words are true?
Should people be held responsible for the words they use?

TIME LINE

1890–1910

1920

1899
John the Baptist (J.B.) Stradford arrives in Tulsa.

1906
Ottowa W. (O.W.) Gurley moves to Tulsa.

1910
Greenwood becomes part of the city of Tulsa.

1921
Black shoe-shiner Dick Rowland is accused of assaulting Sarah Page, a white elevator operator on May 30. He is arrested and held at Tulsa courthouse. On May 31, an editorial appears in the newspaper, angering citizens. Armed Black veterans arrive at the courthouse to protect Rowland in case of a lynching. White citizens also congregate at courthouse.

On June 1, White mobs enter Greenwood overnight, shooting Black residents and setting fire to buildings. Airplanes drop incendiary material onto buildings, setting them ablaze. By midday, the Governor of Oklahoma declares martial law. National Guard troops enter Tulsa. On June 3, martial law is lifted, and a federal investigation is ordered.

1922
Hundreds of buildings are rebuilt in Greenwood and more than eighty businesses are established.

1925
The National Negro Business League holds its annual conference in Greenwood.

Do you think all white Tulsans were racist?
Can a person be racist if they don't participate in things such as looting or lynching?
What is the effect of a white person's inaction or silence in the presence of racism?

How would you explain why the Greenwood Massacre occurred?
Who do you think is responsible?
Should the families that suffered from the event be repaid?

1940   **1960**   **1990**   **2000s**

1942
Over 200 Black-owned businesses have been established in the Greenwood area of Tulsa.

1960s
Historian Don Ross begins investigating the history of the Greenwood Massacre.

1995
Journalists investigating the Oklahoma City bombing meet with Ross and look into the Massacre.

2001
The City of Tulsa Reconciliation report calls for reparations, among other things.

2010
John Hope Franklin Reconciliation Park is developed in Greenwood to remember the victims of the Massacre.

2020
The state of Oklahoma introduces the Massacre to the school curriculum.

amendments (uh-MEND-munts)
Amendments are changes that are made to a law or legal document. The 13th Amendment to the U.S. Constitution declared slavery to be illegal. The 14th Amendment defined who was a citizen of the United States. The 15th Amendment gave Black men the right to vote.

annex (uh-NEKS)
To annex is to add on to something, such as adding a small town to a larger town. In 1910, Greenwood was annexed by Tulsa.

assault (uh-SULT)
An assault is any act of violence that one person commits against another. The word is often understood to mean inappropriate sexual contact.

Black Wall Street
The Greenwood district of Tulsa, Oklahoma was nicknamed "Black Wall Street." It was named after the busy, bustling, and prosperous Wall Street area of New York City.

detention camps (duh-TEN-shun KAMPS)
Places where a government holds, or detains, large groups of people, often in poor conditions.

editorial (ed-ih-TOR-ee-ull)
An editorial is an article in a newspaper or magazine that reflects the writer's opinion.

emancipation (ee-man-sih-PAY-shun)
Emancipation is the freeing of someone from another person's control. Many white people were unhappy with the emancipation of Black people from slavery.

immunity (im-MYOON-ih-tee)
When someone in a legal case is granted immunity, he or she is protected by the court from being held responsible (being punished) for something.

Jim Crow laws
These laws enforced separation of the races in the South. They lasted from the 1870s through the 1950s. Jim Crow was a character demeaning to Black people in a stage performance that began in 1828.

Ku Klux Klan (KOO KLUKS KLAN)
The Ku Klux Klan is a hate group that believes white people of certain religions are better than other people. The Ku Klux Klan has committed many acts of violence against Black people and other people.

Land Run of 1889
A time when land in Utah that had belonged to native tribes was given to Americans to settle.

looting (LOOT-ing)
Looting is the destroying and stealing of property, often as part of a crowd.

lynching (LIN-ching)
A lynching is a mob killing, usually a group of whites murdering a Black man or woman.

martial law (MARSH-ull LAHW)
In times of war or disaster, the army can be called in to control an area and restore order. The Governor of Oklahoma declared martial law at the height of the Greenwood violence.

mob (MAHB)
A mob is a destructive group of people who act together to harm people or property.

Red Summer
A period in 1919, just after the first World War, of increased race-based violence in the U.S.

reparations (rep-uh-RAY-shunz)
Reparations are payments made to people who have been wronged in order to make things right again.

segregation (seh-gruh-GAY-shun)
Segregation is the practice of using laws to keep people apart. Segregation separated Black people and whites in the South for many years.

BOOKS

Buckley, James, Jr. *Who Was Booker T. Washington?*
New York, NY: Penguin Workshop, 2018.

Collier, Christopher and Collier, James Lincoln. *Reconstruction and the Rise of Jim Crow: 1864-1896*. Ashland, OR: Blackstone Publishing, 2012.

Fremon, David K. *The Jim Crow Laws and Racism in American History.* New York, NY: Enslow, 2000.

Latham, Jennifer. *Dreamland Burning*. New York, NY: Little, Brown Books for Young Readers, 2017.

WEBSITES

Visit our website for links about the Tulsa Race Massacre:

childsworld.com/links

Note to Parents, Teachers, and Librarians: We routinely verify our Web links to make sure they are safe, active sites—so encourage your readers to check them out!

INDEX